100

words every
high school
freshman
should know

THE **100** WORDS™ *From the Editors of the*
AMERICAN HERITAGE®
DICTIONARIES

HOUGHTON MIFFLIN

Boston   New York

Visit our websites: www.ahdictionary.com
or www.houghtonmifflinbooks.com

ISBN-13: 978-0-618-44379-6
ISBN-10: 0-618-44379-7

LIBRARY OF CONGRESS CATALOGING-IN-PUBLICATION DATA
100 words every high school freshman should know / by the editors of the
American heritage dictionaries.
    p. cm.
ISBN 0-618-44379-7
    1. Vocabulary—Juvenile literature. I. Title: One hundred words every high
school freshman should know.

PE1449.A144 2004
428.1—dc22

                                                    2003067539

Text design by Anne Chalmers

MANUFACTURED IN THE UNITED STATES OF AMERICA

QUM 10 9 8 7 6 5 4 3 2

Drawings on pages 14 (top) and 44–45 by Robin Storesund.
Drawing on page 14 (bottom) by Academy Artworks.
Drawing on page 25 by Laurel Cook Lhowe.

Table of Contents

**One Hundred Words
Every High School Freshman
Should Know**

Preface

The editors of the *American Heritage* dictionaries are pleased to present the second book in our "100 Words" series, *100 Words Every High School Freshman Should Know.* The words we've chosen are ones that students entering high school should have mastered or are likely to encounter in their studies during their freshman year based on our analysis of textbooks and vocabulary books used in grades seven and eight. The items constitute a well-balanced mix of terms from A to Z, combining straightforward vocabulary items, such as *eclectic, formidable,* and *impertinent,* with words taken directly from areas of study, such as *polygon* and *ellipse* from mathematics and *antibody* and *marsupial* from biology.

Entries, based on the content of the *American Heritage* dictionaries, are presented in an expanded layout that is easy to read and comprehend. In addition to the definitions, we have included additional example sentences to provide greater context. Similarly, we show quotations from a mix of widely assigned works by contemporary authors like Gary Paulsen (*Hatchet*), Maya Angelou (*I Know Why the Caged Bird Sings*), and John Knowles (*A Separate Peace*) as well as classic novelists such as Charlotte Brontë (*Jane Eyre*), Charles Dickens (*Oliver Twist*), and Lewis Carroll (*Alice in Wonderland*). Engaging notes provide background information for some of the scientific vocabulary and delve into the fascinating histories of many other words. To encourage study skills, we have provided exercises at the end of this book for improving vocabulary and encouraging active use of the dictionary.

The first book in the "100 Words" series, *100 Words Every High School Graduate Should Know*, has generated an enormous amount of interest—visitors to our website, www.ahdictionary.com, have viewed the selected words hundreds of thousands of times. We have been delighted by the enthusiastic response and are encouraged by the fact that parents, teachers, and students are taking a strong interest in using dictionaries as an integral part of literacy and vocabulary building. We hope that you will enjoy learning (or learning more about) the words in *100 Words Every High School Freshman Should Know* and that you will find expanding your vocabulary to be a rewarding experience.

Steve Kleinedler,
Senior Editor

Guide to the Entries

THIS GUIDE EXPLAINS THE CONVENTIONS
USED IN THIS BOOK.

ENTRY WORD The 100 words that constitute this book are listed alphabetically. The entry words, along with inflected and derived forms, are divided into syllables by centered dots. These dots show you where you would break the word at the end of a line. The pronunciation of the word follows the entry word. Please see the key on page xi for an explanation of the pronunciation system.

PART OF SPEECH At least one part of speech follows each entry word. The part of speech tells you the grammatical category that the word belongs to. Parts of speech include *noun, adjective, adverb, transitive verb,* and *intransitive verb*. (A transitive verb is a verb that needs an object to complete its meaning. *Wash* is a transitive verb in the sentence *I washed the car*. The direct object of *wash* is *the car*. An intransitive verb is one that does not take an object, as *sleep* in the sentence *I slept for seven hours*. Many verbs are both transitive and intransitive.)

INFLECTIONS A word's inflected forms differ from the main entry form by the addition of a suffix or by a change in the base form to indicate grammatical features such as number, person, or tense. Inflected forms are set in boldface type, divided into syllables, and given pronunciations as necessary. The past tense, past participle, and the third person singular present tense inflections of all verbs are shown. The plurals of nouns are shown when they are spelled in a way other than by adding 's' to the base form.

ORDER OF SENSES Entries having more than one sense are arranged with the central and often the most commonly sought meanings first. In an entry with more than one part of speech, the senses are numbered in separate sequences after each part of speech, as at **flourish.**

EXAMPLES OF USAGE Examples often follow the definitions and are set in italic type. These examples show the entry words in typical contexts. Sometimes the examples are quotations from authors of books. These quotations are shown within quotation marks, and the quotation's author and source are shown.

RELATED WORDS At the end of many entries, additional boldface words appear without definitions. These words are related in basic meaning to the entry word and are usually formed from the entry word by the addition of a suffix.

NOTES Many entries include additional information about the entry words. Some notes explain a scientific concept in greater detail, as at **hologram** and **ozone**. Other notes provide information about the background or history of a word, as at **quarantine** and **yacht**.

EXERCISES At the end of this book, there is a section containing exercises designed to help you further strengthen your vocabulary.

Pronunciation Guide

Pronunciations appear in parentheses after boldface entry words. If a word has more than one pronunciation, the first pronunciation is usually more common than the other, but often they are equally common. Pronunciations are shown after inflections and related words where necessary.

Stress is the relative degree of emphasis that a word's syllables are spoken with. An unmarked syllable has the weakest stress in the word. The strongest, or primary, stress is indicated with a bold mark (ˈ). A lighter mark (ʹ) indicates a secondary level of stress. The stress mark follows the syllable it applies to. Words of one syllable have no stress mark because there is no other stress level that the syllable can be compared to.

The key on page xi shows the pronunciation symbols used in this book. To the right of the symbols are words that show how the symbols are pronounced. The letters whose sound corresponds to the symbols are shown in boldface.

The symbol (ə) is called *schwa*. It represents a vowel with the weakest level of stress in a word. The schwa sound varies slightly according to the vowel it represents or the sounds around it:

a·bun·dant (ə-bŭnʹdənt)   **mo·ment** (mōʹmənt)

civ·il (sĭvʹəl)   **grate·ful** (grātʹfəl)

PRONUNCIATION KEY

Symbol	Examples	Symbol	Examples
ă	pat	oi	noise
ā	pay	ŏŏ	took
âr	care	ŏŏr	lure
ä	father	ōō	boot
b	bib	ou	out
ch	church	p	pop
d	deed, milled	r	roar
ĕ	pet	s	sauce
ē	bee	sh	ship, dish
f	fife, phase,	t	tight, stopped
	rough	th	thin
g	gag	*th*	this
h	hat	ŭ	cut
hw	which	ûr	urge, term,
ĭ	pit		firm, word,
ī	pie, by		heard
îr	deer, pier	v	valve
j	judge	w	with
k	kick, cat, pique	y	yes
l	lid, needle	z	zebra, xylem
m	mum	zh	vision,
n	no, sudden		pleasure,
ng	thing		garage
ŏ	pot	ə	about, item,
ō	toe		edible,
ô	caught,		gallop,
	paw		circus
ôr	core	ər	butter

"Hello," Danny Saunders said softly. "I'm sorry if I woke you. The nurse told me it was all right to wait here."

I looked at him in amazement. He was the last person in the world I had expected to visit me in the hospital. . . .

He smiled sadly, "Can I sit down? I've been standing here about fifteen minutes waiting for you to wake up."

I sort of nodded or did something with my head, and he took it as a sign of approval and sat down on the edge of the bed to my right. The sun streamed in from the windows behind him, and shadows lay over his face and **accentuated** the lines of his cheeks and jaw.

—Chaim Potok,
The Chosen

1

ac·cen·tu·ate (ăk-sĕnt′chŏō-āt′)

transitive verb

    Past participle and past tense: **ac·cen·tu·at·ed**
    Present participle: **ac·cen·tu·at·ing**
    Third person singular present tense: **ac·cen·tu·ates**

1. To give prominence to; emphasize or intensify: *"The sun streamed in from the windows behind him, and shadows lay over his face and accentuated the lines of his cheeks and jaw"* (Chaim Potok, *The Chosen*). **2.** To pronounce with a stress or accent: *accentuate the second syllable in a word.* **3.** To mark with an accent mark: *accentuate a word in a line of poetry.*

RELATED WORD:
    noun —**ac·cen′tu·a′tion**

2

al·lit·er·a·tion (ə-lĭt′ə-rā′shən)

noun

The repetition of the same sounds, usually consonants or consonant clusters, especially at the beginning of words. Poets and writers often employ alliteration in their writing, such as *"I have <u>stood still</u> and <u>stopped</u> the sound of feet"* in Robert Frost's "Acquainted with the Night."

RELATED WORD:
> *adjective* — **al·lit′er·a·tive**

3

a·nal·o·gy (ə-năl′ə-jē)

noun
> Plural: **a·nal·o·gies**

1. Similarity in some respects between things that are otherwise unlike. **2.** An explanation of something by comparing it with something similar: *The author uses the analogy of a beehive when describing the bustling city.*

RELATED WORDS:
> *adjective* — **a·nal′o·gous** (ə-năl′ə-gəs)
> *adverb* — **a·nal′o·gous·ly**

4

an·ti·bod·y (ăn′tĭ-bŏd′ē)

noun

Plural: **an·ti·bod·ies**

A protein produced in the blood or tissues in response to the presence of a specific toxin, foreign blood cell, or other antigen. Antibodies provide immunity against certain microorganisms and toxins by binding with them and often by deactivating them.

📖 **NOTE:** Antibodies are complex, Y-shaped protein molecules that guard our bodies against diseases. The immune system's B lymphocytes, or B cells, develop into plasma cells, which can produce a huge variety of antibodies, each one capable of grabbing an invading molecule at the top ends of the Y. The molecules that antibodies recognize can be quite specific — they might exist only on a particular bacterium or virus. When that bacterium or virus enters the body, the antibodies quickly recognize its molecules, as if a sentry recognized an enemy soldier from his uniform. Once the invader is caught, the antibodies may make it inactive or lead it to cells that can destroy it. High numbers of a particular antibody may persist for months after an infection. The numbers may then get quite small, but the experienced B cells can quickly make more of that specific antibody if necessary. Vaccines work by training B cells to do just that.

5
as·pire (ə-spīr′)

transitive verb

Past participle and past tense: **as·pired**
Present participle: **as·pir·ing**
Third person singular present tense: **as·pires**

To have a great ambition; desire strongly: *aspire to become a good soccer player; aspire to great knowledge.*

RELATED WORDS:
noun — **as′pi·ra′tion**
noun — **as·pir′er**

6
bam·boo·zle (băm-boō′zəl)

transitive verb

Past participle and past tense: **bam·boo·zled**
Present participle: **bam·boo·zling**
Third person singular present tense: **bam·boo·zles**

Informal
To deceive by elaborate trickery; hoodwink: *In* The Music Man, *the con man bamboozles the citizens of River City into believing that he can teach their children to play in a marching band.*

7
bi·zarre (bĭ-zär′)

adjective

Very strange or odd: *a bizarre hat; a bizarre idea.*

RELATED WORD:
    adverb — **bi·zarre′ly**

8
bois·ter·ous (boi′stər-əs *or* boi′strəs)

adjective

1. Rough and stormy; violent: *boisterous winds.* **2.** Noisy and lacking restraint or discipline: *the boisterous cheers of an excited crowd.*

RELATED WORDS:
    adverb — **bois′ter·ous·ly**
    noun — **bois′ter·ous·ness**

9

boy·cott (boi′kŏt′)

transitive verb

   Past participle and past tense: **boy·cott·ed**
   Present participle: **boy·cott·ing**
   Third person singular present tense: **boy·cotts**

To act together in refusing to use, buy from, or deal with, especially as an expression of protest: *boycott a store; boycott foreign-made goods.*

noun

1. A refusal to buy from or deal with a person, business, or nation, especially as a form of protest. **2.** A refusal to buy or use a product or service.

༄ **NOTE:** Even though his name is now a word in English as well as many other languages around the world, Charles C. Boycott probably did not enjoy becoming so famous. He was an English rent-collector in 19th-century Ireland who refused to lower the high rents that Irish farmers paid to English landowners, and he evicted families who could not pay. In 1880, as part of the struggle for Irish independence from the British Empire, people decided to ignore Boycott and his family completely. The servants stopped showing up for work, the mailman would not deliver the mail, and no one would sell the Boycotts anything in the stores. After the success of the *boycott* of Mr. Boycott in Ireland, his name quickly became the usual word for this way of raising protest without resorting to violence.

10

cam·ou·flage (kăm/ə-fläzh/ or kăm/ə-fläj/)

noun

1. A method of concealing military troops or equipment by making them appear to be part of the natural surroundings. **2.** Protective coloring or a disguise that conceals: *An alligator's camouflage makes it look like a log floating in the water.* **3.** Cloth or other material used for camouflage.

transitive verb
> Past participle and past tense: **cam·ou·flaged**
> Present participle: **cam·ou·flag·ing**
> Third person singular present tense: **cam·ou·flag·es**

To conceal or hide by camouflage.

11

chro·nol·o·gy (krə-nŏl/ə-jē)

noun
> Plural: **chro·nol·o·gies**

1. The order or sequence of events: *The lawyer disputed the chronology of events preceding the murder.* **2.** A list or table of events analyzed in order of time of occurrence: *a detailed chronology of modern history.*

RELATED WORDS:
> *adjective* — **chron/o·log/i·cal**
> (krŏn/ə-lŏj/ĭ-kəl)
> *adverb* — **chron/o·log/i·cal·ly**

12

com·mem·o·rate (kə-měm′ə-rāt′)

transitive verb

Past participle and past tense: **com·mem·o·rat·ed**
Present participle: **com·mem·o·rat·ing**
Third person singular present tense:
   com·mem·o·rates

1. To honor the memory of (someone or something), especially with a ceremony: *The crowd gathered in the park to commemorate the firefighters' sacrifice.* **2.** To be a memorial to, as a holiday, ceremony, or statue: *Independence Day commemorates the adoption of the Declaration of Independence.*

RELATED WORDS:
   noun—**com·mem′o·ra′tion**
   adjective—**com·mem′o·ra·tive**
   adverb—**com·mem′o·ra·tive·ly**

13

cow·er (kou′ər)

intransitive verb

Past participle and past tense: **cow·ered**
Present participle: **cow·er·ing**
Third person singular present tense: **cow·ers**

To crouch or draw back, as from fear or pain; cringe: *"Then the dwarves forgot their joy and their confident boasts of a moment before and cowered down in fright"* (JRR Tolkien, *The Hobbit*).

The dwarves were still passing the cup from hand to hand and talking delightedly of the recovery of their treasure, when suddenly a vast rumbling woke in the mountain underneath as if it was an old volcano that had made up its mind to start eruptions once again. The door behind them was pulled nearly to, and blocked from closing with a stone, but up the long tunnel came the dreadful echoes, from far down in the depths, of a bellowing and a trampling that made the ground beneath them tremble.

Then the dwarves forgot their joy and their confident boasts of a moment before and **cowered** down in fright. Smaug was still to be reckoned with. It does not do to leave a live dragon out of your calculations.

— JRR Tolkien,
The Hobbit

14
de·cor·um (dǐ-kôr′əm)

noun

Proper behavior or conduct; propriety: *"She had pull with the police department, so the men in their flashy suits and fleshy scars sat with churchlike decorum and waited to ask favors from her"* (Maya Angelou, *I Know Why The Caged Bird Sings*).

15
de·duc·tion (dǐ-dŭk′shən)

noun

1. The act of subtracting; subtraction: *The sales clerk's deduction of the cost of installation persuaded us to buy the dishwasher.* **2.** An amount that is or may be subtracted: *She claimed a deduction from her taxable income for medical expenses.* **3.** The process of reaching a conclusion by reasoning, especially from general principles. **4.** A conclusion reached by this process: *The article discusses the judge's deduction that the law violated the Fourteenth Amendment.*

16
deign (dān)

verb

> Past participle and past tense: **deigned**
> Present participle: **deign·ing**
> Third person singular present tense: **deigns**

intransitive verb

To be willing to do something that one considers beneath one's dignity; condescend: *"'We better hurry or we'll be late for dinner,' I said . . . [H]is right foot flashed into the middle of my fast walk and I went pitching forward into the grass. 'Get those one hundred and fifty pounds off me!' I shouted, because he was sitting on my back. Finny got up, patted my head genially, and moved on across the field, not deigning to glance around for my counterattack . . ."* (John Knowles, *A Separate Peace*).

transitive verb

To condescend to give: *The movie star didn't deign so much as a nod in our direction.*

de·spon·dent (dĭ-spŏn′dənt)

adjective

Feeling depression of spirits from loss of hope, confidence, or courage; dejected: "*It rained. The procession of weary soldiers became a bedraggled train, despondent and muttering, marching with churning effort in a trough of liquid brown mud under a low, wretched sky*" (Stephen Crane, *The Red Badge of Courage*).

RELATED WORDS:
> *noun*—**de·spon′dence, de·spon′den·cy**
> *adverb*—**de·spon′dent·ly**

di·a·logue (*also spelled* di·a·log) (dī′ə-lôg′)

noun

1. A conversation between two or more people: *a friendly dialogue between neighbors.* **2.** The words spoken by the characters of a play or story: *The dialogue of the comedy was very witty.* **3.** A literary work written in the form of a conversation: *Many students of philosophy have read the dialogues of Plato.* **4.** An exchange of ideas or opinions: *a lively dialogue among members of the committee.*

19

di·vulge (dĭ-vŭlj′)

transitive verb

Past participle and past tense: **di·vulged**
Present participle: **di·vulg·ing**
Third person singular present tense: **di·vulg·es**

To make known; reveal; tell: *divulge a secret.*

RELATED WORD:
  noun — **di·vulg′er**

20

e·clec·tic (ĭ-klĕk′tĭk)

adjective

Choosing or taking what appears to be the best from various sources: *an eclectic musician blending elements of classical music, jazz, and punk rock.*

RELATED WORD:
  adverb — **e·clec′ti·cal·ly**

el·lipse (ĭ-lĭps′)

noun

A figure that forms a closed curve shaped like an oval with both ends alike. An ellipse can be formed by intersecting a cone with a plane that is not parallel or perpendicular to the cone's base. (See top illustration.) The sum of the distances of any point on an ellipse from two fixed points (called the *foci*) remains constant no matter where the point is on the curve. (See bottom illustration.)

THREE-
DIMENSIONAL
ELLIPSE

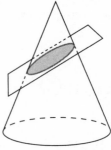

TWO-
DIMENSIONAL
ELLIPSE

The line running through the foci (*F* and *F₁*) of an ellipse is the major axis. The vertices (*V* and *V₁*) mark where the major axis intersects the ellipse.

em·bar·go (ĕm-bär′gō)

noun

Plural: **em·bar·goes**

1. An order by a government prohibiting merchant ships from entering or leaving its ports. **2.** A prohibition by a government on certain or all trade with a foreign nation.

transitive verb

Past participle and past tense: **em·bar·goed**
Present participle: **em·bar·go·ing**
Third person singular present tense: **em·bar·goes**

To place an embargo on: *The Union government embargoed Confederate ports during the Civil War.*

en·thu·si·as·tic (ĕn-thōō′zē-ăs′tĭk)

adjective

Having or showing great interest or excitement: *The principal gave an enthusiastic welcome to the new teachers.*

RELATED WORD:

adverb — **en·thu′si·as′ti·cal·ly**

24

ex·po·nent (ĭk-spō′nənt *or* ĕk′spō′nənt)

noun

1. A number or symbol, placed to the right of and above the expression to which it applies, that indicates the number of times a mathematical expression is used as a factor. For example, the exponent 3 in 5^3 indicates $5 \times 5 \times 5$; the exponent 2 in $(x + y)^2$ indicates $(x + y) \times (x + y)$. **2.** A person who speaks for, represents, or advocates something: *exponents of mass transit as a way of reducing pollution.*

RELATED WORDS:

    adjective—**ex′po·nen′tial**
    adverb—**ex′po·nen′tial·ly**

25

ex·ult (ĭg-zŭlt′)

intransitive verb
    Past participle and past tense: **ex·ult·ed**
    Present participle: **ex·ult·ing**
    Third person singular present tense: **ex·ults**

To rejoice greatly; be jubilant or triumphant: *"Laurie threw up his hat, then remembered that it wouldn't do to exult over the defeat of his guests, and stopped in the middle of the cheer to whisper to his friend, 'Good for you, Jo! He did cheat, I saw him'"* (Louisa May Alcott, *Little Women*).

"Yankees have a trick of being generous to their enemies," said Jo, with a look that made the lad redden, "especially when they beat them," she added, as, leaving Kate's ball untouched, she won the game by a clever stroke.

Laurie threw up his hat, then remembered that it wouldn't do to **exult** over the defeat of his guests, and stopped in the middle of the cheer to whisper to his friend, "Good for you, Jo! He did cheat, I saw him. We can't tell him so, but he won't do it again, take my word for it."

—Louisa May Alcott,
Little Women

fal·la·cy (făl′ə-sē)

noun
Plural: **fal·la·cies**

A false notion or mistaken belief: *It is a fallacy that being popular always means being happy.*

RELATED WORDS:
adjective—**fal·la′cious** (fə-lā′shəs)
adverb—**fal·la′cious·ly**

27

flour·ish (flûr′ĭsh)

verb

> Past participle and past tense: **flour·ished**
> Present participle: **flour·ish·ing**
> Third person singular present tense: **flour·ish·es**

intransitive verb

1. To grow or develop well or luxuriantly; thrive: *Most flowers flourish in full sunlight.* **2.** To do well; prosper: *The lawyer's practice flourished.* **3.** To be actively working, especially in a period of great accomplishment: *a writer who flourished in the later 1600s.*

transitive verb

To wave (something) vigorously or dramatically: *The athletes on the winning team flourished their medals in front of the cameras.*

noun

1. A dramatic action or gesture: *The teacher waved the report with a flourish.* **2.** An added decorative touch; an embellishment: *handwriting with many graceful flourishes.* **3.** In music, a showy passage or a fanfare: *Trumpets played a flourish before the king entered.*

for·mi·da·ble (fôr′mĭ-də-bəl *or* fôr-mĭd′ə-bəl)

adjective

1. Arousing fear, dread, alarm, or great concern: *"The men wish to purchase straw field hats to protect themselves from your formidable Arkansas sun"* (Bette Greene, *The Summer of My German Soldier*). **2.** Admirable; awe-inspiring: *a formidable musical talent.* **3.** Difficult to surmount, defeat, or undertake: *The new assignment was a formidable challenge for the young reporter.*

RELATED WORDS:
    noun — **for′mid·a·bil′i·ty**
    adverb — **for′mi·da·bly**

When the nine prisoners were gathered around the counter the corporal shouted, "Reiker!"

Reiker didn't look quite so tall or strong as the others. His eyes, specked with green, sought communication with my father.

"The men wish to purchase straw field hats to protect themselves from your **formidable** Arkansas sun."

— Bette Greene,
   The Summer of My German Soldier

29

gar·goyle (gär'goil')

noun

A waterspout or ornamental figure in the form of a grotesque animal or person projecting from the gutter of a building.

30

guer·ril·la (*also spelled* gue·ril·la) (gə-rĭl'ə)

noun

A member of a military force that is not part of a regular army and operates in small bands in occupied territory to harass the enemy, as by surprise raids.

31
gu·ru (gŏŏr'ōō)

noun
    Plural: **gu·rus**

1. A Hindu spiritual teacher. **2.** A person who is followed as a leader or teacher.

32
her·i·tage (hĕr'ĭ-tĭj)

noun

1. Something other than property passed down from preceding generations; a tradition: *"We will win our freedom because the sacred heritage of our nation and the eternal will of God are embodied in our echoing demands"* (Martin Luther King, Jr., *Letter from Birmingham Jail*). **2.** Property that is or can be inherited.

hi·er·o·glyph·ic (hī′ər-ə-glĭf′ĭk *or* hī′rə-glĭf′ĭk)

adjective

Of or related to a system of writing, such as that of ancient Egypt, in which pictures or symbols are used to represent words or sounds: *The ancient tombs of the Pharaohs are marked with hieroglyphic writing.*

noun

1. A picture or symbol used in hieroglyphic writing; a hieroglyph. **2.** *often* **hieroglyphics** Hieroglyphic writing, especially that of the ancient Egyptians.

RELATED WORDS:
> *noun*—**hi′er·o·glyph′**
> *adverb*—**hi′er·o·glyph′i·cal·ly**

✍ **NOTE:** *Hieroglyphic* comes from a Greek word meaning "sacred carvings." *Hieros* meant "sacred" in Greek, and *glyphein* meant "to carve." Although the Egyptians wrote hieroglyphs on papyrus and painted them on walls, the Greeks who visited Egypt must have been more impressed by the stately carvings on the stones of immense temples and tombs. The Egyptians' own

---

word for their writing system was *mdw nṯr*, "words of the god." You could pronounce this (mĕd′ōō nĕch′ĕr). The Egyptians thought the gods themselves used these symbols, which possessed great power. When they wrote hieroglyphs showing dangerous animals, such as snakes, on the walls of their tombs, they would sometimes leave the symbols unfinished — or even damage them intentionally. This would prevent the hieroglyphs from coming alive and harming the person entombed there.

The Egyptians enclosed the names of royalty in an oval shape called a *cartouche*. This oval represented the circular path of the sun around the world, and so indicated that the pharaoh was ruler of "all that the sun encircles."

Below is the full name of one of the greatest pharaohs, Ramses II, written in its original Egyptian form.

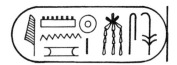

hol·o·gram (hŏl′ə-grăm′ *or* hō′lə-grăm′)

noun

The photographic record of a three-dimensional image produced by recording on a photographic plate or film the pattern of interference formed by a split laser beam. The plate or film is then illuminated with a laser or with ordinary light to form the image.

> **NOTE:** If you tear an ordinary photograph in two, each piece shows only a part of the original image. If you break a *hologram* in two, each piece shows the entire original scene, although from slightly different points of view. That's because each spot on a hologram contains enough information to show how the entire scene would look if it were viewed from a particular point of view. Imagine looking at a room through a peephole set in a solid door. What you see depends on where in the door the peephole is placed. Each piece of the hologram is a "peephole" view, and that's what makes the image look three-dimensional: as you move the hologram around or look at different parts of it, you see the original object from different angles, just as if you were walking around it. For this reason, holograms are much harder to copy than simple two-dimensional images, because to forge one you'd have to know what the original object looked like from many angles. And that's why credit cards and other important items include stickers bearing holograms as indicators of authenticity.

35

hy·poc·ri·sy (hĭ-pŏk′rĭ-sē)

noun

The practice of showing or expressing feelings, beliefs, or virtues that one does not actually hold or possess.

RELATED WORD:
noun — **hyp′o·crite′** (hĭp′ə-krĭt′)

36

im·mune (ĭ-myōōn′)

adjective

1. Protected from disease naturally or by vaccination or inoculation: *I'm immune to chickenpox because I had it when I was young.* **2.** Not subject to an obligation imposed on others; exempt: *As a diplomat, he is immune from criminal prosecution.* **3.** Not affected by a given influence; unresponsive: *"I am immune to emotion. I have been ever since I can remember. Which is helpful when people appeal to my sympathy. I don't seem to have any"* (Ellen Wittlinger, *Hard Love*).

RELATED WORD:
verb — **im′mu·nize′** (ĭm′yə-nīz′)

im·per·ti·nent (ĭm-pûr′tn-ənt)

adjective

1. Offensively bold; rude: "'*I don't like the look of it at all,*' *said the King:* '*however, it may kiss my hand if it likes.*' '*I'd rather not,*' *the Cat remarked.* '*Don't be impertinent,*' *said the King,* '*and don't look at me like that!*'" (Lewis Carroll, *Alice's Adventures in Wonderland*). **2.** Not pertinent; irrelevant: *The discussion went on for hours because of the many impertinent questions and remarks.*

RELATED WORD:

     adverb — **im·per′ti·nent·ly**

"Who *are* you talking to?" said the King, coming up to Alice, and looking at the Cat's head with great curiosity.

"It's a friend of mine — a Cheshire Cat," said Alice: "allow me to introduce it."

"I don't like the look of it at all," said the King: "however, it may kiss my hand if it likes."

"I'd rather not," the Cat remarked.

"Don't be **impertinent**," said the King, "and don't look at me like that!" He got behind Alice as he spoke.

"A cat may look at a king," said Alice. "I've read that in some book, but I don't remember where."

— Lewis Carroll,
Alice's Adventures in Wonderland

in·fer·ence (ĭn′fər-əns)

noun

1. The act or process of deciding or concluding by reasoning from evidence: *arrive at a logical conclusion by inference.* **2.** Something that is decided or concluded by reasoning from evidence; a conclusion: *The evidence is too scanty to draw any inferences from it.*

> ✍ **NOTE:** When we say that a speaker or sentence makes an **implication** or **implies** something, we mean that it is indicated or suggested without being stated outright: *Even though you say you like sports, your lack of enthusiasm implies that you don't.* To make an **inference** about something or **infer** something, on the other hand, is to draw conclusions that are not stated openly in what is said: *I infer from your lack of enthusiasm that you don't like sports.*

RELATED WORD:
   verb — **in·fer′**

in·tro·spec·tion (ĭn′trə-spĕk′shən)

noun

The examination of one's own thoughts and feelings.

RELATED WORDS:
   adjective — **in′tro·spec′tive**
   adverb — **in′tro·spec′tive·ly**

40

jaun·ty (jônt′tē *or* jänt′tē)

adjective
    Comparative: **jaun·ti·er**
    Superlative: **jaun·ti·est**

1. Having or showing a carefree self-confident air: *"A figure was approaching us over the moor, and I saw the dull red glow of a cigar. The moon shone upon him, and I could distinguish the dapper shape and jaunty walk of the naturalist"* (Arthur Conan Doyle, *The Hound of the Baskervilles*). **2.** Stylish or smart in appearance: *a jaunty hat.*

RELATED WORDS:
    adverb — **jaun′ti·ly**
    noun — **jaun′ti·ness**

41

jo·vi·al (jō′vē-əl)

adjective

Full of fun and good cheer; jolly: *a jovial host.*

RELATED WORDS:
    noun — **jo′vi·al′i·ty** (jō′vē-ăl′ĭ-tē)
    adverb — **jo′vi·al·ly**

kil·o·me·ter (kĭ-lŏm′ĭ-tər *or* kĭl′ə-mē′tər)

noun

A unit of length equal to 1,000 meters or 0.62 of a mile.

🐾 **NOTE:** The metric system is a system of measurement that is based on the number 10. Because 12 inches make a foot, and 3 feet make a yard, calculating the number of inches in a given number of yards or miles can often be cumbersome. In the metric system, multiplication is easy. *Kilo-* is a prefix meaning "a thousand," so one kilometer is equal to a thousand meters, and one kilogram is equal to a thousand grams. Likewise, if you know something is 18 kilometers away, you can easily calculate that it's 18,000 meters away.

Some common prefixes in the metric system are:

milli-	"one thousandth"	kilo-	"one thousand"
centi-	"one hundredth"	cento-	"one hundred"
deci-	"one tenth"	deca-	"ten"

The basic units of measurement in the metric system are the *gram*, for weight; the *liter*, for volume; and the *meter*, for distance. The prefixes can be combined with these units to form different measurements: a *centigram* is a hundredth (1/100) of a gram; a *milliliter* is a thousandth (1/1000) of a liter.

But the metric system isn't limited to these units: a *kilowatt* is a thousand watts, and a *millisecond* is a thousandth of second.

There are even more prefixes for larger and smaller units!

micro-	"one millionth"	mega-	"one million"
nano-	"one billionth"	giga-	"one billion"
pico-	"one trillionth"	tera-	"one trillion"

43
lab·y·rinth (lăb′ə-rĭnth′)

noun

1. A complex structure of connected passages through which it is difficult to find one's way; a maze. **2. Labyrinth** In Greek mythology, the maze built by Daedalus in Crete to confine the Minotaur. **3.** Something complicated or confusing in design or construction. **4.** The system of tubes and spaces that make up the inner ear of many vertebrate animals.

44
la·con·ic (lə-kŏn′ĭk)

adjective

Using few words; terse; concise: *a laconic reply.*

RELATED WORD:
  adverb — **la·con′i·cal·ly**

45
li·chen (lī′kən)

noun

An organism that consists of a fungus and an alga growing in close association with each other. Lichens often live on rocks and tree bark and can also be found in extremely cold environments.

46

light-year (līt′yîr′)

noun

The distance that light travels in one year, about 5.88 trillion miles (9.47 trillion kilometers).

47

ma·neu·ver (mə-nōō′vər)

noun

1. A planned movement of troops or warships: *By a series of brilliant maneuvers, the general outwitted the enemy.* **2.** *often* **maneuvers** A large-scale military exercise in which battle movements are practiced. **3.** A controlled change in movement or direction of a vehicle or vessel, especially an aircraft. **4.** A movement or procedure that involves skill or cunning: *The gymnast made an acrobatic maneuver and landed squarely on the mat.*

verb
> Past participle and past tense: **ma·neu·vered**
> Present participle: **ma·neu·ver·ing**
> Third person singular present tense: **ma·neu·vers**

intransitive verb
1. To change tactics or approach; plan skillfully: *Our lawyer maneuvered in order to get the trial postponed.* **2.** To carry out a military maneuver. **3.** To make controlled changes in movement or direction: *The ship had to maneuver carefully to avoid the icebergs.*

transitive verb

1. To cause (troops or warships) to carry out a military maneuver. **2.** To direct skillfully by changes in course or in position: *"He let me maneuver the skiff through the wreckage of the flood without even peeking over his shoulder to see what I might be about to hit"* (Katherine Paterson, *Jacob Have I Loved*). **3.** To manage or direct, especially by trickery: *She maneuvered her opponent into taking a position that lost him the election.*

RELATED WORDS:

> *noun* — **ma·neu′ver·a·bil′i·ty**
> *adjective* — **ma·neu′ver·a·ble**

48

mar·su·pi·al (mär-sōō′pē-əl)

noun

Any of various mammals, such as the kangaroo, opossum, or wombat, whose young continue to develop after birth in a pouch on the outside of the female's body.

49

met·a·phor (mĕt′ə-fôr′)

noun

A figure of speech in which a word or phrase that is ordinarily associated with one thing is applied to something else, thus making a comparison between the two. For example, when Shakespeare wrote, "All the world's a stage," and "Life's but a walking shadow," he was using metaphors.

50

mo·sa·ic (mō-zā′ĭk)

noun

1. A picture or design made on a surface by fitting and cementing together small colored pieces, as of tile, glass, or stone. **2.** The art or process of making such pictures or designs. **3.** Something that resembles a mosaic: *I tried to understand the mosaic of impressions the author had after visiting Mexico.* **4.** A viral disease of certain plants, such as tobacco or tomatoes, that causes the leaves to become spotted or wrinkled.

51

mu·ta·tion (myōō-tā′shən)

noun

1. A change in a gene or chromosome of an organism that can be inherited by its offspring. **2.** The process by which such a change occurs. **3.** An organism or individual that has undergone such a change. **4.** A change, as in form.

RELATED WORD:
  verb — **mu′tate**

52

neb·u·la (nĕb′yə-lə)

noun
  Plural: **neb·u·lae** (nĕb′yə-lē′) *or* **neb·u·las**

A thinly spread cloud of interstellar gas and dust. It will appear as a bright patch in the night sky if it reflects light from nearby stars, emits its own light, or re-emits ultraviolet radiation from nearby stars as visible light. If it absorbs light, the nebula appears as a dark patch. In dark nebulae, stars form from clumps of hydrogen gas.

RELATED WORD:
  adjective — **neb′u·lar**

There were three circumstances in particular which made me think that its [The Morlocks'] rare emergence above ground was the outcome of a long-continued underground look common in most animals that live largely in the dark —the white fish of the Kentucky caves, for instance. Then, those large eyes, with that capacity for reflecting light, are common features of **nocturnal** things —witness the owl and the cat. And last of all, that evident confusion in the sunshine, that hasty yet fumbling awkward flight towards dark shadow, and that peculiar carriage of the head while in the light — all reinforced the theory of an extreme sensitiveness of the retina.

—H.G. Wells,
The Time Machine

53

noc·tur·nal (nŏk-tûr**′**nəl)

adjective

1. Of, relating to, or occurring at night: *a nocturnal breeze.* **2.** Active at night: *"[T]hose large eyes, with that capacity for reflecting light, are common features of nocturnal things—witness the owl and the cat"* (H. G. Wells, *The Time Machine*).

RELATED WORD:
    adverb — **noc·tur′nal·ly**

54

nui·sance (nōō**′**səns)

noun

A source of inconvenience or annoyance; a bother.

om·ni·vore (ŏm′nə-vôr′)

noun

An organism that eats both plants and animals.

𝒷𝒶 **NOTE:** Our word *omnivore* comes from Latin *omnivorus*, "eating everything." Like many scientific words that English has borrowed from Latin, *omnivore* is a compound—a single word made by putting two other words together. The first part of the Latin word, *omni-*, means "all" or "every." The second part, *-vorus*, means "eating, swallowing." We can find this same root *-vor-* at the end of several other English words. For example, *carnivore* means literally "meat-eating." Here we see *-vor-* added to the same *carn-* as in *chili con carne*, "chili with meat." *Herbivore*, meaning "plant eater," has the same *herb-* as in *herbal tea*. The English verb *devour* comes from Latin *dēvorāre*, which also contains the root *-vor-*. The same root is found at the beginning of yet another word in this book, *voracious*, from Latin *vorāx*, "ravenous."

out·ra·geous (out-rā′jəs)

adjective

Exceeding all bounds of what is right or proper; immoral or offensive: *an outrageous crime; outrageous prices.*

RELATED WORD:
> *adverb* — **out·ra′geous·ly**
> *noun* — **out·ra′geous·ness**

o·zone (ō′zōn′)

noun

A poisonous, unstable form of oxygen that has three atoms per molecule rather than the usual two. It is produced by electricity and is present in the air, especially after a thunderstorm. Commercially, it is produced for use in water purification, air conditioning, and as a bleaching agent.

NOTE: For the earth's organisms, including people, *ozone* can be a lifesaver or a threat to health, depending on how high it is found in the atmosphere. The ozone that lingers in the lower atmosphere is a pollutant and contributes to respiratory diseases like asthma. But in the upper atmosphere, ozone protects us from the more severe forms of the sun's radiation. The region of the atmosphere in which ozone is most concentrated is known as the *ozone layer,* which lies from about 10 to 20 miles (16 to 32 kilometers) above the earth. Because ozone absorbs certain wavelengths of harmful ultraviolet radiation, this layer acts as an important protection for life on the earth. In recent years the ozone has thinned or disappeared in parts of the ozone layer, especially over the polar regions, creating ozone "holes" that let in dangerous amounts of ultraviolet radiation. Ozone holes are created in part by the presence of certain industrial or commercial chemicals released into the atmosphere.

par·a·site (păr′ə-sīt′)

noun

1. An organism that lives in or on a different kind of organism from which it gets nourishment and to which it is sometimes harmful. Lice and tapeworms are parasites. **2.** A person who takes advantage of the generosity of others without making any useful return.

par·ti·ci·ple (pär′tĭ-sĭp′əl)

noun

A verb form that is used with auxiliary verbs to indicate certain tenses and that can also function as an adjective. The present participle is indicated by *–ing*, as in *running* and *sleeping.* The past participle is usually indicated by *–ed*, as in *walked* and *nailed*, but many English verbs have irregular past participles, such as *fought, sung,* and *known.* Past participles are also used to make the passive voice: *The board was nailed to the wall.*

 **NOTE:** You should always avoid the "dangling" participle, as in the sentence *Turning the corner, the view was quite different.* This sentence is constructed so that it seems that the present participle *turning* modifies the noun *view.* As you read the sentence, you might at first think that the view is turning the corner. You should rewrite such sentences: *The view was quite different when we turned the corner,* or *Turning the corner, we saw a different view.*

60

phlo·em (flō'ĕm')

noun

A plant tissue that conducts food from the leaves to the other plant parts. Phloem consists primarily of tube-like cells that have porous openings. In mature woody plants it forms a sheathlike layer of tissue in the stem, just inside the bark.

61

pla·teau (plă-tō')

noun
  Plural: **pla·teaus** *or* **pla·teaux** (plă-tōz')

1. An elevated, comparatively level expanse of land. **2.** A relatively stable level or stage of growth or development: *The economy has reached a new plateau.*

pol·y·gon (pŏl′ē-gŏn′)

noun

A flat, closed geometric figure bounded by three or more line segments. Triangles, rectangles, and octagons are all examples of polygons.

RELATED WORD:
 adjective— **po·lyg′o·nal** (pə-lĭg′ə-nəl)

EXAMPLES OF POLYGONS

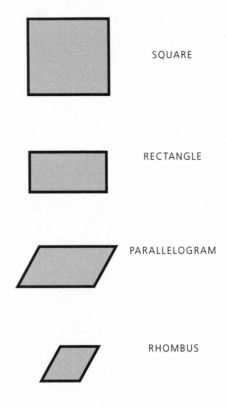

SQUARE

RECTANGLE

PARALLELOGRAM

RHOMBUS

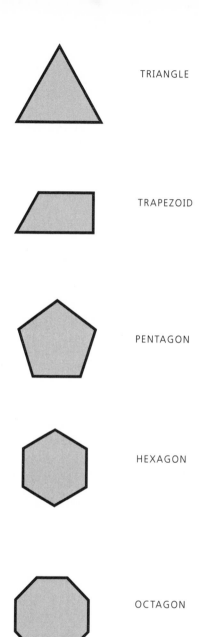

TRIANGLE

TRAPEZOID

PENTAGON

HEXAGON

OCTAGON

63
pro·tag·o·nist (prō-tăg′ə-nĭst)

noun

The main character in a drama or literary work.

64
pul·ver·ize (pŭl′və-rīz′)

verb
> Past participle and past tense: **pul·ver·ized**
> Present participle: **pul·ver·iz·ing**
> Third person singular present tense: **pul·ver·iz·es**

transitive verb
To pound, crush, or grind to powder or dust: *"He felt that the stars had been pulverized by the sound of the black jets and that in the morning the earth would be covered with their dust like a strange snow"* (Ray Bradbury, *Fahrenheit 451*).

intransitive verb
To be ground or reduced to powder or dust.

RELATED WORD:
> *noun* — **pul′ver·i·za′tion** (pŭl′vər-ĭ-zā′shən)

He felt that the stars had been **pulverized** by the sound of the black jets and that in the morning the earth would be covered with their dust like a strange snow. That was his idiot thought as he stood shivering in the dark, and let his lips go on moving and moving.

—Ray Bradbury,
Fahrenheit 451

65

quan·da·ry (kwŏn′də-rē *or* kwŏn′drē)

noun
    Plural: **quan·da·ries**

A condition of uncertainty or doubt; a dilemma: *I'm in a quandary over what to do next.*

66

quar·an·tine (kwŏr′ən-tēn′)

noun

A condition, period of time, or place in which a person or animal is confined or kept in isolation in an effort to prevent a disease from spreading.

transitive verb
    Past participle and past tense: **quar·an·tined**
    Present participle: **quar·an·tin·ing**
    Third person singular present tense: **quar·an·tines**

To keep (someone or something) confined or isolated, especially as a way to keep a disease from spreading; place (someone or something) in quarantine.

🐚 **NOTE:** The word *quarantine* comes from Italian *quarantina*, "a group of forty"—in this case, a group of forty days. The word originally described the number of days in which a newly arrived ship was kept in isolation, a practice begun in Venice and other port cities as a defense against the plague. The Italian word for "forty," *quaranta*, may remind you of words in other languages you may know, such as French *quarante* or Spanish *cuarenta*. They all descend from Latin *quadrāgintā*, "forty." The first part of this word, *quadr-*, means "four," and we can find it in many other English words. A *quadrangle* has four angles. A *squadron* was originally a group of soldiers in *square* (that is, four-sided) formation. A *quarry* was a place where stone was cut into blocks with square sides.

quo·ta (kwō′tə)

noun

1. An amount of something assigned, as to be done, made, or sold: *a machine shop's production quota.* **2.** A number or percentage, especially of people, that represents an upper limit: *strict immigration quotas.* **3.** A number or percentage, especially of people, that represents a required or targeted minimum: *a system of quotas for hiring minority applicants.*

rain·for·est (*also spelled* **rain forest**) (rān′fôr′ĭst)

noun

A dense evergreen forest with an annual rainfall of at least 160 inches (406 centimeters).

🖉 **NOTE:** Rainforests are, not surprisingly, forests where it rains a lot—between 160 and 400 inches (406 and 1,016 centimeters) a year. Most of the world's rainforests lie near the equator and have tropical climates. However, there are also cooler rainforests, such as the one in the northwest United States and southwestern Canada along the Pacific Ocean. The largest rainforest, covering as much territory as the rest of the world's rainforests combined, is in the Amazon River basin in South America. Rainforests are extremely important because they help regulate the world's climate and because they contain a wider variety of plants and animals than any other environment on the earth. Among the many benefits of this biodiversity is its support of important biological research. For example, many of the natural chemicals used in prescription drugs are found in plants that grow only in rainforests.

69
ran·dom (răn′dəm)

adjective

Having no specific pattern, purpose, or objective: *the random movements of leaves falling from the trees.*

idiom
at random
Without a method or purpose; unsystematically: *Choose a card at random from the deck.*

RELATED WORD:
> *adverb* — **ran′dom·ly**
> *noun* — **ran′dom·ness**

70
re·cede (rĭ-sēd′)

intransitive verb
> Past participle and past tense: **re·ced·ed**
> Present participle: **re·ced·ing**
> Third person singular present tense: **re·cedes**

1. To move back or away from a limit, degree, point, or mark: *The floodwaters receded from the streets.* **2.** To grow less or diminish, as in intensity: *"[H]e stood and held his abdomen until the hunger cramps receded"* (Gary Paulsen, *Hatchet*). **3.** To slope backward: *a man with a chin that recedes.* **4.** To become fainter or more distant: *Over the years his memory of that summer receded.*

He stood, went back to the water, and took small drinks. As soon as the cold water hit his stomach, he felt the hunger sharpen, as it had before, and he stood and held his abdomen until the hunger cramps **receded**.

He had to eat. He was weak with it again, down with the hunger, and he had to eat.

—Gary Paulsen,
Hatchet

ren·ais·sance (rĕn′ĭ-säns′ *or* rĕn′ĭ-säns′)

noun

1. A rebirth or revival: *a renaissance of downtown business.* **2. Renaissance** The revival of classical art, literature, architecture, and learning in Europe that occurred from the 14th through the 16th century.

adjective

Renaissance Of or relating to the Renaissance or its artistic works or styles.

𝒫 NOTE: When the Roman Empire crumbled in the middle of the fifth Century, literate people in Western Europe took refuge in monasteries, where they contemplated the nature of God and prepared for the next world. The art and literature of the ancient Greeks and Romans, and the values that they expressed, were largely forgotten or ignored, because of their pagan origins. During the centuries just after the collapse of the empire, it was difficult to pass on knowledge from the past because of the great decline in living conditions. Then in the fourteenth and fifteenth centuries, a new interest was kindled the achievements of Greece and Rome—first in Italy and then spreading to the rest of Western Europe. A thousand years after the fall of Rome, the fall of another empire helped bring about a revival of classical civilization in the West. The Greeks of the Byzantine Empire had preserved manuscripts of classical literature and the knowledge of how to read them. As the Byzantine Empire crumbled and finally fell to the Turks in 1453, Greek scholars fled as refugees to Italy, and manuscripts were brought to western Europe for preservation. When western scholars and artists examined the great achievements of Greece and Rome, they found new inspiration to create art and literature for their own age. In its vibrancy and vitality, this age was like a new birth for European culture, and so we now call it the Renaissance.

ren·e·gade (rĕn′ĭ-gād′)

noun

1. A person who rejects a cause, allegiance, religion, or group for another. **2.** An outlaw.

adjective

Of, relating to, or resembling a renegade; traitorous.

re·pose (rĭ-pōz′)

noun

1. The act of resting or the state of being at rest. **2.** Peace of mind; freedom from anxiety: *seeking security and repose.* **3.** Calmness; tranquility: *"It was the cool gray dawn, and there was a delicious sense of repose and peace in the deep pervading calm and silence of the woods"* (Mark Twain, *The Adventures of Tom Sawyer*).

verb
>   Past participle and past tense: **re·posed**
>   Present participle: **re·pos·ing**
>   Third person singular present tense: **re·pos·es**

transitive verb
To lay (oneself) down to rest.

intransitive verb
1. To lie at rest; relax or sleep. **2.** To lie supported by something: *a dish reposing on the table.*

When Tom awoke in the morning, he wondered where he was. He sat up and rubbed his eyes and looked around. Then he comprehended. It was the cool gray dawn, and there was a delicious sense of **repose** and peace in the deep pervading calm and silence of the woods. Not a leaf stirred; not a sound obtruded upon great Nature's meditation. Beaded dewdrops stood upon the leaves and grasses. A white layer of ashes covered the fire, and a thin blue breath of smoke rose straight into the air. Joe and Huck still slept.

— Mark Twain,
The Adventures of Tom Sawyer

sac·ri·fice (săk′rə-fīs′)

noun

1. The act of giving up something highly valued for the sake of something else considered to be of greater value: *He was willing to make sacrifices in order to become a musician.* **2.** The act of offering something, such as an animal's life, to a deity in worship or to win favor or forgiveness. **3.** A victim offered this way. **4.** In baseball: **a.** A bunt that allows a runner to advance a base while the batter is retired. **b.** A fly ball enabling a runner to score after it is caught by a fielder.

verb

> Past participle and past tense: **sac·ri·ficed**
> Present participle: **sac·ri·fic·ing**
> Third person singular present tense: **sac·ri·fic·es**

transitive verb

1. To offer (something or someone) as a sacrifice to a deity. **2.** To give up (one thing) for another thing considered to be of greater value.

intransitive verb

1. To make or offer a sacrifice. **2.** In baseball, to hit a sacrifice bunt or sacrifice fly.

RELATED WORD:
> *adjective* — **sac′ri·fi′cial** (săk′rə-fĭsh′əl)

---

sil·hou·ette (sĭl′ōo-ĕt′)

noun

1. A drawing consisting of the outline of something, especially a human profile, filled in with a solid color. **2.** An outline of something that appears dark against a light background: *"A storm was coming up from the south, moving slowly. It looked something like a huge blue-gray shower curtain being drawn along by the hand of God. You could just barely see through it, enough to make out the silhouette of the mountains on the other side"* (Barbara Kingsolver, *The Bean Trees*).

transitive verb
>Past participle and past tense: **sil·hou·et·ted**
>Present participle: **sil·hou·et·ting**
>Third person singular present tense: **sil·hou·ettes**

To cause to be seen as a silhouette: *The lamp silhouetted his profile against the window shade.*

76

sol·stice (sŏl′stĭs *or* sōl′stĭs)

noun

Either of the times of year when the sun is farthest north or south of the equator. In the Northern Hemisphere, the summer solstice occurs on June 20 or 21 and the winter solstice occurs on December 21 or 22.

77

spec·trum (spĕk′trəm)

noun

Plural: **spec·tra** (spĕk′trə) *or* **spec·trums**

1. A band of colors seen when white light is broken up according to wavelengths, as when passing through a prism or striking drops of water. **2.** The entire range of electromagnetic radiation, from gamma rays, which have the shortest wavelengths and highest frequencies, to radio waves, which have the longest wavelengths and lowest frequencies. Visible light, with intermediate wavelengths and frequencies, is near the center of the electromagnetic spectrum. **3.** A broad range of related qualities, ideas, or activities: *This class will cover a wide spectrum of ideas.*

ster·e·o·type (stĕr′ē-ə-tīp′)

noun

A conventional or oversimplified idea or image: *the stereotype of the meek librarian.*

transitive verb
   Past participle and past tense: **ster·e·o·typed**
   Present participle: **ster·e·o·typ·ing**
   Third person singular present tense: **ster·e·o·types**

To make a stereotype of: *a movie that stereotypes farmers as unsophisticated.*

RELATED WORD:
   noun — **ster′e·o·typ′er**

strat·e·gy (străt′ə-jē)

noun
   Plural: **strat·e·gies**

1. The science of using all the forces of a nation as effectively as possible during peace or war. **2.** A plan of action arrived at by means of this science or intended to accomplish a specific goal.

RELATED WORD:
   adjective — **stra·te′gic** (strə-tē′jĭk)

suf·frage (sŭf'rĭj)

noun

The right to vote in political elections: *Susan B. Anthony campaigned for women's suffrage.*

sym·bi·o·sis (sĭm'bē-ō'sĭs *or* sĭm'bī-ō'sĭs)

noun

Plural: **sym·bi·o·ses** (sĭm'bē-ō'sēz' *or* sĭm'bī-ō'sēz')

The close association between two or more different organisms of different species, often but not necessarily benefiting each member.

🐾 **NOTE:** Two organisms that live together in **symbiosis** may have one of three kinds of relationships: *mutualism, commensalism,* or *parasitism.* The *mutualism* shown by the rhinoceros and the tickbird benefits both. Riding on the rhino's back, the tickbird eats its fill of the ticks that bother the rhino while the rhino gets warning calls from the bird when it senses danger. In *commensalism,* one member benefits and the other is unaffected. The ocean fish known as the remora attaches to a shark by a suction disk on its head and gets to eat the scraps left after the shark feeds. But the shark is unaffected by the remora's presence. In *parasitism,* though, one species generally gets hurt, as when fleas infest a dog's coat and feed on its blood.

82
tar·iff (tăr′ĭf)

noun

1. A tax or duty imposed by a government on a category of imported or exported goods, such as automobiles or steel. **2.** A list or system of these taxes or duties. **3.** A list or table of prices or fees.

83
tech·nique (tĕk-nēk′)

noun

1. A procedure or method for accomplishing a complicated task, as in a science or an art: *a new technique for making computer chips.* **2.** Skill in handling such procedures or methods: *As a pianist, she has nearly perfect technique.*

84
tem·po (tĕm′pō)

noun
　　Plural: **tem·pos** *or* **tem·pi** (tĕm′pē)

1. The speed at which music is or ought to be played. **2.** A characteristic rate or rhythm of something; a pace: *the rapid tempo of life in a city.*

tox·in (tŏk′sĭn)

noun

A poisonous substance produced by a living organism. Toxins can be products of ordinary metabolism (such as those found in urine), can be produced to kill or immobilize prey (such as the toxins in snake venom), or can be produced for self-defense (such as the cyanide produced by several plants). Toxins produced by bacteria cause disease.

RELATED WORD:
 adjective — **tox′ic**

tran·quil·i·ty (*also spelled* **tran·quil·li·ty**)
(trăng-kwĭl′ĭ-tē *or* trăn-kwĭl′ĭ-tē)

noun

The quality or condition of being free from disturbance; calmness; serenity: "*We the people of the United States, in order to form a more perfect union, establish justice, insure domestic tranquility . . . do ordain and establish this Constitution for the United States of America*" (Preamble to the Constitution of the United States of America).

We the people of the United States, in order to form a more perfect union, establish justice, insure domestic **tranquility**, provide for the common defense, promote the general welfare, and secure the blessings of liberty to ourselves and our posterity, do ordain and establish this Constitution for the United States of America.

— Preamble to the
Constitution of the
United States of America

tu·mult (tōo′mŭlt′)

noun

1. Noisy and disorderly activity; a commotion or disturbance; an uproar. **2.** Emotional or mental commotion or agitation.

RELATED WORD:
    adjective—**tu·mul′tu·ous** (tŏo-mŭl′chōo-əs)

tun·dra (tŭn′drə)

noun

A cold, treeless, usually lowland area of far northern regions. The subsoil of tundras is permanently frozen, but in summer the top layer of soil thaws and can support low-growing mosses, lichens, grasses, and small shrubs: *"As I looked about me at the stark and cloud-topped hills, the waste of pressure-rippled ice, and, beyond the valley, to the desolate and treeless roll of tundra, I had no doubt that this was excellent wolf country"* (Farley Mowatt, *Never Cry Wolf*).

"As I looked about me at the stark and cloud-topped hills, the waste of pressure-rippled ice, and, beyond the valley, to the desolate and treeless roll of **tundra**, I had no doubt that this was excellent wolf country. Indeed, I suspected that many pairs of lupine eyes were already watching me with speculative interest. I burrowed into my mountain of gear, found the revolver, and then took stock of the situation."

— Farley Mowatt,
Never Cry Wolf

ul·tra·vi·o·let (ŭl′trə-vī′ə-lĭt)

adjective

Of or relating to electromagnetic radiation having wavelengths shorter than those of visible light but longer than those of x-rays.

u·nan·i·mous (yōō-năn′ə-məs)

adjective

1. Sharing the same opinion; being fully in agreement: *"[N]eighborhood opinion was unanimous that Mrs. Dubose was the meanest old woman who ever lived"* (Harper Lee, *To Kill a Mockingbird*). **2.** Based on or characterized by complete agreement: *a unanimous vote.*

RELATED WORD:
    adverb — **u·nan′i·mous·ly**

Cecil Jacobs, who lived at the far end of our street next door to the post office, walked a total of one mile per school day to avoid the Radley Place and old Mrs. Henry Lafayette Dubose. Mrs. Dubose lived two doors up the street from us; neighborhood opinion was **unanimous** that Mrs. Dubose was the meanest old woman who ever lived.

— Harper Lee,
To Kill a Mockingbird

un·du·late (ŭn′jə-lāt′)

intransitive verb

    Past participle and past tense: **un·du·lat·ed**
    Present participle: **un·du·lat·ing**
    Third person singular present tense: **un·du·lates**

1. To move in waves or with a smooth wavy motion: *wheat undulating in the breeze.* **2.** To have a wavy appearance or form: *A line undulated across the chalkboard.*

RELATED WORD:
    noun — **un′du·la′tion**

vac·cine (văk-sēn′)

noun

A substance that stimulates cells in the immune system to recognize and attack disease-causing agents, especially through the production of antibodies. Most vaccines are given by injection or are swallowed as liquids. Vaccines may contain a weaker form of the disease-causing virus or bacterium or even a DNA fragment or some other component of the agent.

RELATED WORD:
> *noun* — **vac′ci·na′tion**

🐾 **NOTE:** The word *vaccine* ultimately comes from Latin *vacca*, "cow," a word that may be familiar to you as French *vache* or Spanish *vaca*. Before the days of vaccination, the dread disease smallpox had long been a leading cause of death all over the world. In 1796, however, the English doctor Edward Jenner noticed that people who had caught cowpox, a mild disease contracted from dairy cows, did not get smallpox afterwards. Jenner took liquid from the cowpox sores of a milkmaid and injected a boy with it. Later, Jenner exposed the boy to smallpox, but the boy did not get sick. In this way, Jenner had discovered a safe way to prevent smallpox. From the Latin name for cowpox, *variolae vaccīnae* (literally, "smallpox of cows"), Jenner's technique became known as *vaccination*, and the liquid he injected as *vaccine.*

vac·il·late (văs′ə-lāt′)

intransitive verb

Past participle and past tense: **vac·il·lat·ed**
Present participle: **vac·il·lat·ing**
Third person singular present tense: **vac·il·lates**

To be unable to decide between one opinion or course of action and another; waver: *I vacillated between going on vacation with my family or going to summer camp.*

RELATED WORD:
   noun—**vac′il·la′tion**

ver·te·brate (vûr′tə-brĭt *or* vûr′tə-brāt′)

noun

Any of a large group of animals having a backbone, including the fishes, amphibians, reptiles, birds, and mammals.

adjective

1. Having a backbone: *vertebrate animals.* **2.** Of or characteristic of a vertebrate or vertebrates: *the vertebrate brain.*

---

vir·tu·o·so (vûr′chōō-ō′sō *or* vûr′chōō-ō′zō)

noun

Plural: **vir·tu·o·sos** *or* **vir·tu·o·si** (vûr′chōō-ō′sē)

1. A musical performer of great excellence, technique, or ability. **2.** A person of great skill or technique: *a chef who was a virtuoso in the kitchen.*

adjective

Exhibiting the ability, technique, or personal style of a virtuoso: *a virtuoso performance.*

vo·ra·cious (və-rā′shəs)

adjective

1. Eating or eager to eat great amounts of food; ravenous: *"Oliver Twist and his companions suffered the tortures of slow starvation for three months: at last they got so voracious and wild with hunger, that one boy . . . hinted darkly to his companions, that unless he had another basin of gruel per diem, he was afraid he might some night happen to eat the boy who slept next him…"* (Charles Dickens, *Oliver Twist*). **2.** Having or marked by an insatiable appetite for an activity or occupation: *a voracious reader.*

RELATED WORDS:

> *adverb*—**vo·ra′cious·ly**
> *noun*—**vo·ra′cious·ness**

Boys have generally excellent appetites. Oliver Twist and his companions suffered the tortures of slow starvation for three months: at last they got so **voracious** and wild with hunger, that one boy, who was tall for his age, and hadn't been used to that sort of thing (for his father had kept a small cook-shop), hinted darkly to his companions, that unless he had another basin of gruel *per diem*, he was afraid he might some night happen to eat the boy who slept next him, who happened to be a weakly youth of tender age. He had a wild, hungry eye; and they implicitly believed him. A council was held; lots were cast who should walk up to the master after supper that evening, and ask for more; and it fell to Oliver Twist.

— Charles Dickens,
Oliver Twist

wretch·ed (rĕch′ĭd)

adjective
> Comparative: **wretch·ed·er** *or* **more wretched**
> Superlative: **wretch·ed·est** *or* **most wretched**

1. Very unhappy or unfortunate; miserable: *a wretched prisoner.* **2.** Characterized by or causing distress or unhappiness: *"But my night was wretched, my rest broken: the ground was damp, the air cold: besides, intruders passed near me more than once, and I had again and again to change my quarters: no sense of safety or tranquillity befriended me"* (Charlotte Brontë, *Jane Eyre*). **3.** Hateful or contemptible: *a bigot with a wretched personality.* **4.** Inferior in quality: *The movie was wretched.*

RELATED WORDS:
> *adverb* — **wretch′ed·ly**
> *noun* — **wretch′ed·ness**

I could not hope to get a lodging under a roof, and sought it in the wood I have before alluded to. But my night was **wretched**, my rest broken: the ground was damp, the air cold: besides, intruders passed near me more than once, and I had again and again to change my quarters: no sense of safety or tranquillity befriended me. Towards morning it rained; the whole of the following day was wet. Do not ask me, reader, to give a minute account of that day; as before, I sought work; as before, I was repulsed; as before, I starved; but once did food pass my lips. At the door of a cottage I saw a little girl about to throw a mess of cold porridge into a pig trough. "Will you give me that?" I asked.

— Charlotte Brontë,
Jane Eyre

98
xy·lem (zī′ləm)

noun

A plant tissue that carries water and dissolved minerals up from the roots through the stem to the leaves and provides support for the softer tissues. Xylem consists of various elongated cells that function as tubes. In a tree trunk, the innermost part of the wood is dead but structurally strong xylem.

99
yacht (yät)

noun

Any of various relatively small sailing or motor-driven vessels used for pleasure trips or racing.

NOTE: Many English words related to the sea or seafaring are borrowed from Dutch, including *brackish, corvette, deck, dock, freebooter, harpoon, hoist, maelstrom, mesh* (of a net), *reef, school* (of fish), *skipper, sloop, tackle, trawl,* and *walrus.* The word *yacht,* the only common English word in which *ch* is silent, was probably borrowed from Dutch *jaght,* now spelled *jacht.* Norwegian also has the word *jakt,* related to Dutch *jacht,* and possibly both languages contributed to the development of English *yacht.* These words ultimately come from Middle Low German *jachtschip,* or "hunting ship." The original Dutch *jacht,* a fast, light boat, actually served the practical purposes of pursuing smugglers. In 1660, the Dutch East India Company gave Charles II of England a *jacht* of this type. However, he used it for pleasure *cruises*—another word from Dutch!

In Dutch, the *ch* is actually pronounced as a separate sound, like the one you make when you clear your throat—it is like the *ch* at the end of the German pronunciation of the composer *Bach.* English used to have this sound, too. Everyone is familiar with silent *gh* from words such as *bought* and *thought.* This silent *gh* once spelled the same throat-clearing sound, which disappeared in English in the sixteenth century. By the time the English borrowed the Dutch word *jacht,* they could no longer say the *ch* very well, so it was left out of the pronunciation. But the spelling of the word stayed the same.

zo·ol·o·gy (zō-ŏl′ə-jē *or* zōō-ŏl′ə-jē)

noun

Plural: **zo·ol·o·gies**

1. The branch of biology that deals with animals. **2.** The animals of a particular area or period: *Australia is very different from the zoology of North America.*

Exercises
to Improve and
Enrich Your Vocabulary

Knowing and being able to use the *100 Words Every High School Freshman Should Know* is just one step that you can take to expand your vocabulary. Along with a good dictionary, such as the *American Heritage® Student Dictionary* or the *American Heritage® High School Dictionary*, you can use these 100 words as a starting point to discover new words. The exercises shown below are among the many ways you can become more familiar with your dictionary and improve your vocabulary.

Building your vocabulary is an ongoing process that you can continue throughout your life. If you feel discouraged because you can't retain the definitions of all the words that you encounter, approach the task of expanding your vocabulary more slowly. If learning ten words a week is too difficult, aim for three, or five.

What is important is not the quantity of words you're learning. Rather, what is important is your process behind learning the words and the commitment you make to yourself to strengthen your vocabulary over time.

Choose ten words from the list of *100 Words Every High School Freshman Should Know*. Look these ten words up in your dictionary.

On each page that these ten words are listed, choose a new word whose meaning you do not know. Create a document on your computer and type in that word along with its definition, or write the word down on paper with its definition.

For example, other words appearing on the same page as **bamboozle** in the *American Heritage Student Dictionary* that you might choose to learn include **balsam, balustrade,** or **banal**.

Keep a record of the new words that you learn. Every so often, go back and refresh your memory by rereading the definitions to these words. Create sentences that use these words so that you can become comfortable using them.

EXERCISE II

Choose a magazine or newspaper that you like to read at least once a week. Create a document on your computer or start a journal in a notebook. Every time you read a word whose meaning you're unsure of, add that word to your computer file or journal entry.

Look up the word in your dictionary, and write or type out the definition. Does knowing the precise definition of the word help you understand the article?

After you have acquired a list of ten words, memorize them until they are part of your active vocabulary.

EXERCISE III

Many of the words in the list of *100 Words Every High School Freshman Should Know* include terms from specific areas of study. For example, **ellipse** and **polygon** are both from the field of geometry. **Antibody** and **mutation** are from biology.

What fields of learning interest you? Create a list of ten words that you think people should know if they were to learn more about that topic. Think about how you would define those words, and compare your definitions with the definitions you find in your dictionary.